Vegan Cookbook for Millenial

Recipes for a balanced and healthy diet

By Rollo Biefer

Sommario

Introduction

Many people consider vegetarianism as a lifestyle that in addition to respecting animals also has other important advantages such as a great reduction in the risk of chronic diseases and diabetes. mainly they are divided into two strands, in fact there are some of them who prefer to consume at least products of animal origin and others who, instead, taking their beliefs to the extreme, prefer to eliminate even those and are called vegans. in both cases the choice is made to abolish all forms of meat including chicken, beef, game and fish. At this point I recommend that you go in search of your favorite dish in our fantastic book, Bon Appetite.

Main Course

Grilled Carrot, Turnip and Water Chestnuts with Balsamic Glaze

Ingredients

1 large carrots, peeled and cut
lengthwise1 large turnip, peeled and

cut lengthwise 1/2 cup canned water chestnuts

2 pcs. Portobello mushrooms, rinsed and drainedDressing Ingredients

6 tbsp. extra virgin olive oilSea salt, to taste

3 tbsp. Balsamic vinegar1 tsp. Dijon mustard

Marinate the vegetable with the dressing or marinade ingredients for15 to 30 min.

Grill for 4 minutes over medium heat or until the vegetable becomestender.

Grilled Water Chestnuts and Mangoes

Ingredients

1/2 cup water chestnuts

2 large mangoes, cut lengthwise and pitted
Dressing Ingredients

6 tbsp. sesame
oilSea salt, to
taste

3 tbsp. distilled white
vinegar1 tsp. Egg-free
mayonnaise

Marinate the vegetable with the dressing or marinade
ingredients for15 to 30 min.

Grill for 4 minutes over medium heat or until the vegetable
becomestender.

For the mango, grill only until you start seeing brown grill marks.

Grilled beetroots and Green Beans

Ingredients

2 beetroots, peeled and sliced lengthwise

1 medium Pineapple, cut into 1/2 inch
slices10 Green Beans

2 large red onions, cut into ½ inch rings but don't
separate intoindividual rings

Dressing

Ingredients6 tbsp.
olive oil

Sea salt, to taste

3 tbsp. white wine
vinegar1 tsp. English
mustard

Marinate the vegetable with the dressing or marinade
ingredients for15 to 30 min.

Grill for 4 minutes over medium heat or until the vegetable
becomestender.

Grilled Artichoke Hearts and Water Chestnuts

Ingredients

½ cup canned artichoke hearts1/2 cup water chestnuts

10 pcs. Brussel Sprouts

Dressing Ingredients6 tbsp. olive oil

Sea salt, to taste

3 tbsp. white wine vinegar 1 tsp. Egg-free mayonnaise

Marinate the vegetable with the dressing or marinade ingredients for15 to 30 min.

Grill for 4 minutes over medium heat or until the vegetable becomestender.

Grilles Turnips Broccolini and Water Chestnuts with Honey Apple Cider Glaze

Ingredients

10 Broccolini Florets

1/2 cup water

chestnuts

1 large turnip, peeled and cut lengthwise

Dressing Ingredients

6 tbsp. extra virgin olive

oilSea salt, to taste

3 tbsp. apple cider

vinegar1 tbsp. honey

1 tsp. Egg-free mayonnaise

Marinate the vegetable with the dressing or marinade ingredients for15 to 30 min.

Grill for 4 minutes over medium heat or until the vegetable

becomestender.

Grilled Assorted Bell Peppers with Broccolini Florets Recipe

Ingredients

1 Green Bell Pepper, cut in half

2 beetroots, peeled and sliced lengthwise1 Red Bell Pepper, cut in half

10 Broccolini Florets

Marinade Ingredients:

6 tbsp. extra virgin olive oilSea salt, to taste

3 tbsp. distilled white vinegar1 tsp. Dijon mustard

Marinate the vegetable with the dressing or marinade ingredients for15 to 30 min.

Grill for 4 minutes over medium heat or until the vegetable becomestender.

Grilled Eggplant & Beetroot with Assorted Bell Peppers

Ingredients

1 small Eggplant, cut lengthwise and cut in half2 beetroots, peeled and sliced lengthwise

1 large turnip, peeled and cut lengthwise1 Yellow Bell Pepper, cut in half

1 Red Bell Pepper, cut in half

Dressing Ingredients6 tbsp. sesame oil Sea salt, to taste

3 tbsp. distilled white vinegar1 tsp. Egg-free mayonnaise

Marinate the vegetable with the dressing or marinade

ingredients for 15 to 30 min.

Grill for 4 minutes over medium heat or until the vegetable becomes tender.

Grilled Portobello and Rutabaga

Ingredients

1 medium Rutabaga, peeled and cut in half
lengthwise5 pcs. Portobello mushrooms, rinsed
and drained

1 medium red onion, cut into ½ inch rings but don't
separate intoindividual rings

Dressing Ingredients

6 tbsp. extra virgin olive
oilSea salt, to taste

3 tbsp. Balsamic
vinegar1 tsp. Dijon
mustard

Marinate the vegetable with the dressing or marinade
ingredients for15 to 30 min.

Grill for 4 minutes over medium heat or until the vegetable

becomestender.

Grilled Water Chestnuts Zucchini and Endives

Ingredients

2 large zucchini , cut lengthwise into ½ inch
slabs1/2 cup water chestnuts

1 bunch of endives
Dressing
Ingredients6 tbsp.
sesame oil Sea
salt, to taste

3 tbsp. distilled white
vinegar1 tsp. Egg-free
mayonnaise

Marinate the vegetable with the dressing or marinade
ingredients for15 to 30 min.

Grill for 4 minutes over medium heat or until the vegetable
becomestender.

Grilled Brussel Sprouts Cauliflower and Rutabaga

Ingredients

1 medium Rutabaga, peeled and cut in half
lengthwise 10 Cauliflower florets

5 pcs. Brussel Sprouts

1 bunch of collard greens

Dressing Ingredients 6 tbsp. olive oil

Sea salt, to taste

3 tbsp. white wine
vinegar 1 tsp. English
mustard

Marinate the vegetable with the dressing or marinade ingredients for 15 to 30 min.

Grill for 4 minutes over medium heat or until the vegetable becomes tender.

Grilled Collard Greens Portobello and Asparagus

Ingredients

3 pcs. Portobello, rinsed and drained

1 medium Rutabaga, peeled and cut in half lengthwise1 bunch of collard greens

6 pcs. Asparagus

Dressing

Ingredients6 tbsp.

sesame oil Sea

salt, to taste

3 tbsp. distilled white

vinegar1 tsp. Egg-free

mayonnaise

Marinate the vegetable with the dressing or marinade

ingredients for15 to 30 min.

Grill for 4 minutes over medium heat or until the vegetable

becomestender.

Grilled Water Chestnuts Swiss Chard and Asparagus Recipe

Ingredients

1/2 cup water
chestnuts1 bunch of
swiss chard 6 pcs.
Asparagus

Dressing Ingredients

6 tbsp. extra virgin olive
oilSea salt, to taste

3 tbsp. apple cider
vinegar1 tbsp. honey

1 tsp. Egg-free mayonnaise

Marinate the vegetable with the dressing or marinade
ingredients for15 to 30 min.

Grill for 4 minutes over medium heat or until the vegetable

becomestender.

Grilled Ruttabaga and Swiss Chard

Ingredients

1 medium Rutabaga, peeled and cut in half lengthwise

2 large red onions, cut into ½ inch rings but don't separate intoindividual rings

1 bunch of swiss chard

Marinade Ingredients:

6 tbsp. extra virgin olive
oilSea salt, to taste

3 tbsp. distilled white
vinegar1 tsp. Dijon
mustard

Marinate the vegetable with the dressing or marinade ingredients for15 to 30 min.

Grill for 4 minutes over medium heat or until the vegetable becomestender.

Grilled Asparagus Pineapple and Green Beans

Ingredients

1 medium Rutabaga, peeled and cut in half
lengthwise10 pcs. Asparagus

1 medium Pineapple, cut into 1/2 inch
slices1 bunch of collard greens

Dressing
Ingredients6 tbsp.
sesame oil Sea
salt, to taste

3 tbsp. distilled white
vinegar1 tsp. Egg-free
mayonnaise

Marinate the vegetable with the dressing or marinade
ingredients for15 to 30 min.

Grill for 4 minutes over medium heat or until the vegetable
becomestender.

Grilled Green Beans and Eggplants

Ingredients

2 beetroots, peeled and sliced lengthwise

3 large Zucchinis, cut lengthwise and cut in
  half10 Green Beans

4 Dressing Ingredients

6 tbsp. extra virgin olive
oilSea salt, to taste

3 tbsp. Balsamic
vinegar1 tsp. Dijon
mustard

Marinate the vegetable with the dressing or marinade
ingredients for15 to 30 min.

Grill for 4 minutes over medium heat or until the vegetable
becomestender.

Grilled Asparagus and Broccolini

Ingredients

1 bunch of swiss chard

5 pcs. Portobello mushrooms, rinsed and drained8 pcs. Asparagus

Dressing
Ingredients6 tbsp.
sesame oil Sea
salt, to taste

3 tbsp. distilled white
vinegar1 tsp. Egg-free
mayonnaise

Marinate the vegetable with the dressing or marinade ingredients for15 to 30 min.

Grill for 4 minutes over medium heat or until the vegetable becomestender.

Grilled Collard Greens and Brussel Sprouts

Ingredients

1 bunch of collard greens 10 pcs. Brussel Sprouts 10 Broccolini Florets

1 bunch of swiss chard

Dressing Ingredients 6 tbsp. olive oil

Sea salt, to taste

3 tbsp. white wine vinegar 1 tsp. English mustard

Marinate the vegetable with the dressing or marinade ingredients for 15 to 30 min.

Grill for 4 minutes over medium heat or until the vegetable becomestender.

Grilled Broccoli & Swiss Chard

Ingredients

2 Green Bell Peppers, cut in
half1 bunch of swiss chard

5 Broccoli Florets

Dressing
Ingredients6 tbsp.
sesame oil Sea
salt, to taste

3 tbsp. distilled white
vinegar1 tsp. Egg-free
mayonnaise

Marinate the vegetable with the dressing or marinade
ingredients for15 to 30 min.

Grill for 4 minutes over medium heat or until the vegetable
becomestender.

Grilled Swiss Chard and Asparagus

Ingredients

1 medium Rutabaga, peeled and cut in half lengthwise

2 large red onions, cut into ½ inch rings but don't separate intoindividual rings

1 bunch of swiss
chard10 pcs.
Asparagus

Dressing Ingredients

6 tbsp. extra virgin olive
oilSea salt, to taste

3 tbsp. apple cider
vinegar1 tbsp. honey

1 tsp. Egg-free mayonnaise

Marinate the vegetable with the dressing or marinade
ingredients for15 to 30 min.

Grill for 4 minutes over medium heat or until the vegetable
becomestender.

Grilled Water Chestnuts and Green Beans

Ingredients

10 Broccolini Florets

10 pcs. Asparagus

1/2 cup water
chestnuts 10 Green
Beans

Marinade Ingredients:

6 tbsp. extra virgin olive
oil Sea salt, to taste

3 tbsp. distilled white
vinegar 1 tsp. Dijon
mustard

Marinate the vegetable with the dressing or marinade
ingredients for 15 to 30 min.

Grill for 4 minutes over medium heat or until the vegetable becomestender.

Grilled Endives and Edamame Beans

Ingredients

10 Edamame Beans

2 beetroots, peeled and sliced
lengthwise1 bunch of endives

Dressing
Ingredients6 tbsp.
olive oil

Sea salt, to taste

3 tbsp. white wine
vinegar 1 tsp. Egg-free
mayonnaise

Marinate the vegetable with the dressing or marinade
ingredients for15 to 30 min.

Grill for 4 minutes over medium heat or until the vegetable

becomestender.

Grilled Turnip Greens and Okra

**Ingredie
ns**

5 pcs.
Okra

1 bunch of turnip greens

2 large red onions, cut into ½ inch rings but don't
separate intoindividual rings

Dressing Ingredients

6 tbsp. extra virgin olive
oilSea salt, to taste

3 tbsp. Balsamic
vinegar1 tsp. Dijon
mustard

Marinate the vegetable with the dressing or marinade

ingredients for 15 to 30 min.

Grill for 4 minutes over medium heat or until the vegetable becomestender.

Grilled Water Chestnuts and Cabbage

Ingredients

1 Green cabbage

1/2 cup water chestnuts

2 large red onions, cut into ½ inch rings but don't separate intoindividual rings

2 tbsp. extra virgin olive
oil2 tbsp. ranch dressing
mix

Marinate the vegetable with the dressing or marinade ingredients for15 to 30 min.

Grill for 4 minutes over medium heat or until the vegetable becomestender.

Grilled Beetroots and Purple Cabbage

Ingredients

1 large Parsnip, cut
lengthwise1 Purple cabbage

2 beetroots, peeled and sliced lengthwise

2 large Zucchinis, cut lengthwise and cut in half

Dressing
Ingredients6 tbsp.
olive oil

Sea salt, to taste

3 tbsp. white wine
vinegar1 tsp. English
mustard

Marinate the vegetable with the dressing or marinade
ingredients for15 to 30 min.

Grill for 4 minutes over medium heat or until the vegetable becomestender.

Grilled Okra and Waterchestnuts

Ingredients

1 Red cabbage

1/2 cup water
chestnuts5 pcs. Okra

3 pcs. Asparagus
Corns, cut
lengthwise

2 pcs. Portobello mushrooms, rinsed and drained

Marinade Ingredients:

6 tbsp. extra virgin olive
oilSea salt, to taste

3 tbsp. distilled white
vinegar1 tsp. Dijon
mustard

Marinate the vegetable with the dressing or marinade ingredients for 15 to 30 min.

Grill for 4 minutes over medium heat or until the vegetable becomestender.

Grilled Turnip and Endives

Ingredients

1 large Turnip, cut lengthwise

2 Green Bell Peppers, cut in
half1 bunch of endives

Dressing Ingredients

6 tbsp. extra virgin olive
oilSea salt, to taste

3 tbsp. apple cider
vinegar1 tbsp. honey

1 tsp. Egg-free mayonnaise

Marinate the vegetable with the dressing or marinade
ingredients for15 to 30 min.

Grill for 4 minutes over medium heat or until the vegetable

becomestender.

Grilled Turnip Greens and Broccolini

Ingredients

1 bunch of turnip greens 10 pcs. Brussel Sprouts 10 Broccolini Florets

10 pcs. Asparagus

Dressing Ingredients 6 tbsp. sesame oil Sea salt, to taste

3 tbsp. distilled white vinegar 1 tsp. Egg-free mayonnaise

Marinate the vegetable with the dressing or marinade ingredients for 15 to 30 min.

Grill for 4 minutes over medium heat or until the vegetable

becomestender.

Grilled Green Beans and Pineapple

Ingredients

1 large Turnip, cut lengthwise

1 medium Pineapple, cut into 1/2 inch
slices 10 Green Beans

Dressing
Ingredients 6 tbsp.
sesame oil Sea

salt, to taste

3 tbsp. distilled white
vinegar1 tsp. Egg-free
mayonnaise

Marinate the vegetable with the dressing or marinade
ingredients for15 to 30 min.

Grill for 4 minutes over medium heat or until the vegetable
becomestender.

Grilled Parsnip and Microgreens

Ingredients

1 large Parsnip, cut lengthwise1 bunch of microgreens

2 large red onions, cut into ½ inch rings but don't separate intoindividual rings

Dressing
Ingredients6 tbsp. olive oil

Sea salt, to taste

3 tbsp. white wine vinegar 1 tsp. Egg-free mayonnaise

Marinate the vegetable with the dressing or marinade

ingredients for 15 to 30 min.

Grill for 4 minutes over medium heat or until the vegetable becomes tender.

Grilled Turnip and Zucchini

Ingredients

1 large Turnip, cut
lengthwise1 bunch of
turnip greens

1 large zucchini , cut lengthwise into ½ inch slabs

2 small red onions, cut into ½ inch rings but don't
separate intoindividual rings

Dressing Ingredients

6 tbsp. extra virgin olive
oilSea salt, to taste

3 tbsp. Balsamic
vinegar1 tsp. Dijon
mustard

Marinate the vegetable with the dressing or marinade

ingredients for15 to 30 min.

Grill for 4 minutes over medium heat or until the vegetable becomestender.

Grilled Carrot, Parsnip and Endives

Ingredients

1 large Carrot, cut
lengthwise 1 large Parsnip,
cut lengthwise1 bunch of
endives

10 pcs. Asparagus

10 Green Beans

Dressing
Ingredients6 tbsp.
olive oil

Sea salt, to taste

3 tbsp. white wine
vinegar1 tsp. English
mustard

Marinate the vegetable with the dressing or marinade ingredients for 15 to 30 min.

Grill for 4 minutes over medium heat or until the vegetable becomes tender.

Grilled Portobello Mushrooms and Broccolini Florets

Ingredients

10 Broccolini Florets

10 pcs. Asparagus
Corns, cut
lengthwise

5 pcs. Portobello mushrooms, rinsed and drained

Marinade Ingredients:

6 tbsp. extra virgin olive
oilSea salt, to taste

3 tbsp. distilled white
vinegar1 tsp. Dijon
mustard

Marinate the vegetable with the dressing or marinade
ingredients for15 to 30 min.

Grill for 4 minutes over medium heat or until the vegetable becomestender.

Grilled Cauliflower and Baby Corn

Ingredients

10 Cauliflower florets

½ cup canned baby
corn10 pcs. Brussel
Sprouts

Dressing Ingredients

6 tbsp. extra virgin olive
oilSea salt, to taste

3 tbsp. apple cider
vinegar1 tbsp. honey

1 tsp. Egg-free mayonnaise

Marinate the vegetable with the dressing or marinade
ingredients for15 to 30 min.

Grill for 4 minutes over medium heat or until the vegetable becomestender.

Grilled Beetroots and Artichoke Hearts

Ingredients

½ cup canned artichoke

hearts10 Broccolini Florets

2 beetroots, peeled and sliced lengthwise

Dressing

Ingredients6 tbsp.

sesame oil Sea

salt, to taste

3 tbsp. distilled white

vinegar1 tsp. Egg-free

mayonnaise

Marinate the vegetable with the dressing or marinade ingredients for15 to 30 min.

Grill for 4 minutes over medium heat or until the vegetable

becomestender.

Grilled Baby Carrots and Beetroots

Ingredients

5 pcs. baby carrots

2 large Eggplants, cut lengthwise and cut in
half2 beetroots, peeled and sliced

lengthwise

Dressing
Ingredients6 tbsp.
sesame oil Sea
salt, to taste

3 tbsp. distilled white
vinegar1 tsp. Egg-free
mayonnaise

Marinate the vegetable with the dressing or marinade
ingredients for15 to 30 min.

Grill for 4 minutes over medium heat or until the vegetable
becomestender.

Grilled Baby Carrots and Zucchini

Ingredients

7 pcs. baby carrots

2 large zucchini , cut lengthwise into ½ inch slabs

2 large red onions, cut into ½ inch rings but don't separate intoindividual rings

Dressing
Ingredients6 tbsp.
olive oil

Sea salt, to taste

3 tbsp. white wine
vinegar 1 tsp. Egg-free
mayonnaise

Marinate the vegetable with the dressing or marinade ingredients for15 to 30 min.

Grill for 4 minutes over medium heat or until the vegetable becomestender.

Grilled Microgreens and Beetroots

Ingredients

1 bunch of microgreens

2 beetroots, peeled and sliced
lengthwiseCorns, cut lengthwise

Dressing Ingredients

6 tbsp. extra virgin olive
oilSea salt, to taste

3 tbsp. Balsamic
vinegar1 tsp. Dijon
mustard

Marinate the vegetable with the dressing or marinade
ingredients for15 to 30 min.

Grill for 4 minutes over medium heat or until the vegetable
becomestender.

Grilled Water Chestnuts Baby Carrots and Artichoke Hearts

Ingredients

1 cup canned artichoke
hearts 1/2 cup canned water
chestnuts 8 pcs. baby carrots

Dressing
Ingredients 6 tbsp.
olive oil

Sea salt, to taste

3 tbsp. white wine
vinegar 1 tsp. English
mustard

Marinate the vegetable with the dressing or marinade
ingredients for 15 to 30 min.

Grill for 4 minutes over medium heat or until the vegetable becomestender.

Grilled Rutabaga Pineapple and Artichoke Hearts

Ingredients

1 medium Pineapple, cut into 1/2 inch slices

1 medium Rutabaga, peeled and cut in half
lengthwise1 cup canned artichoke hearts

Marinade Ingredients:

6 tbsp. extra virgin olive
oilSea salt, to taste

3 tbsp. distilled white
vinegar1 tsp. Dijon
mustard

Marinate the vegetable with the dressing or marinade
ingredients for15 to 30 min.

Grill for 4 minutes over medium heat or until the vegetable
becomestender.

Grilled Rutabaga Zucchini and Onions

Ingredients

1 medium Rutabaga, peeled and cut in half lengthwise2 large zucchini , cut lengthwise into ½ inch slabs

2 large red onions, cut into ½ inch rings but don't separate intoindividual rings

Dressing
Ingredients6 tbsp.
olive oil

Sea salt, to taste

3 tbsp. white wine
vinegar 1 tsp. Egg-free
mayonnaise

Marinate the vegetable with the dressing or marinade

ingredients for 15 to 30 min.

Grill for 4 minutes over medium heat or until the vegetable becomestender.

Simple Grilled Water Chestnuts and Cauliflower Florets

Ingredients

1/2 cup canned water chestnuts10 Cauliflower florets

10 pcs. Brussel Sprouts

Dressing Ingredients

6 tbsp. extra virgin olive oilSea salt, to taste

3 tbsp. apple cider vinegar1 tbsp. honey

1 tsp. Egg-free mayonnaise

Marinate the vegetable with the dressing or marinade ingredients for15 to 30 min.

Grill for 4 minutes over medium heat or until the vegetable becomestender.

Grilled Rutabaga Broccolini Florets and Bell Peppers

Ingredients

1 medium Rutabaga, peeled and cut in half
lengthwise2 Green Bell Peppers, cut in half

10 Broccolini Florets

Dressing
Ingredients6 tbsp.
sesame oil Sea
salt, to taste

3 tbsp. distilled white
vinegar1 tsp. Egg-free
mayonnaise

Marinate the vegetable with the dressing or marinade
ingredients for15 to 30 min.

Grill for 4 minutes over medium heat or until the vegetable
becomestender.

Grilled Baby Corn, Water Chestnuts and Eggplant

Ingredients

½ cup canned baby corn

1/2 cup canned water chestnuts

2 large Eggplants, cut lengthwise and cut in half

Dressing
Ingredients6 tbsp.
olive oil

Sea salt, to taste

3 tbsp. white wine
vinegar 1 tsp. Egg-free
mayonnaise

Marinate the vegetable with the dressing or marinade ingredients for15 to 30 min.

Grill for 4 minutes over medium heat or until the vegetable becomestender.

Grilled Baby Carrots and Winter Squash

Ingredients

1 winter squash, peeled and sliced lengthwise

½ cup baby carrots

1 bunch of turnip greens

2 large red onions, cut into ½ inch rings but don't separate intoindividual rings

Dressing Ingredients

6 tbsp. extra virgin olive oilSea salt, to taste

3 tbsp. Balsamic vinegar1 tsp. Dijon mustard

Marinate the vegetable with the dressing or marinade ingredients for15 to 30 min.

Grill for 4 minutes over medium heat or until the vegetable becomestender.

Grilled Broccolini Beetroots and Portobello Mushroom

Ingredients

10 Broccolini Florets

2 beetroots, peeled and sliced lengthwiseCorns, cut lengthwise

5 pcs. Portobello mushrooms, rinsed and drained

Dressing
Ingredients6 tbsp.
sesame oil Sea
salt, to taste

3 tbsp. distilled white
vinegar1 tsp. Egg-free
mayonnaise

Marinate the vegetable with the dressing or marinade ingredients for15 to 30 min.

Grill for 4 minutes over medium heat or until the vegetable becomestender.

Grilled Beetroots and Artichoke Hearts in Viniagrette

Ingredients

1 cup canned artichoke hearts

2 beetroots, peeled and sliced lengthwise

Dressing
Ingredients6 tbsp.
olive oil

Sea salt, to taste

3 tbsp. white wine
vinegar1 tsp. English
mustard

Marinate the vegetable with the dressing or marinade ingredients for15 to 30 min.

Grill for 4 minutes over medium heat or until the vegetable becomestender.

Grilled Baby Carrots and Baby Carrots

Ingredients

10 pcs. Baby Carrots

2 beetroots, peeled and sliced lengthwise

Dressing
Ingredients 6 tbsp.
olive oil

Sea salt, to taste

3 tbsp. white wine
vinegar 1 tsp. Egg-free
mayonnaise

Marinate the vegetable with the dressing or marinade ingredients for 15 to 30 min.

Grill for 4 minutes over medium heat or until the vegetable becomes tender.

Grilled Beetroots Artichoke Hearts and Asparagus

Ingredients

½ cup canned artichoke hearts

2 beetroots, peeled and sliced
lengthwise 10 pcs. Asparagus

Dressing Ingredients

6 tbsp. extra virgin olive
oil Sea salt, to taste

3 tbsp. apple cider
vinegar 1 tbsp. honey

1 tsp. Egg-free mayonnaise

Marinate the vegetable with the dressing or marinade ingredients for 15 to 30 min.

Grill for 4 minutes over medium heat or until the vegetable

becomestender.

Conclusion

Did you enjoy trying these new and delicious recipes?

unfortunately we have come to the end of this vegetarian cookbook, I really hope it has been to your liking.

to improve your health we would like to advise you to combine physical activity and a dynamic lifestyle as well as follow these fantastic recipes, so as to accentuate the improvements. we will be back soon with other increasingly intriguing vegetarian recipes, a big hug, see you soon.

CPSIA information can be obtained
at www.ICGtesting.com
Printed in the USA
BVHW011552040521
606321BV00022B/370